MW00804348

HerLife HerWrite Publishing Co. LLC

ISBN: 978-1-7349232-3-0

Pollinated Pieces

Welcome to the Honey Comb

Hello, world thanks for tuning in for a visual read of my life through poetic expressions. It's my motto to "write it out, until its right out". Poetry became my outlet, after it was discovered around the age of 8. I was a child to let things build inside and have random outbursts. It came out like a storm, and the raging "winds" expressed the "thunder" I felt. I didn't understand how to communicate. I just knew fighting was a way to get out what I felt with my fists. Then, my hands found a new outlet, and "writing it out, until it was right out" happened. My thoughts dripped my feelings from the pen to the pad. Now, I can release my various emotions of happy, angry, or sad. Poetry saved my life; I owe it to the paper to continue to write. "Many are silent and haven't found a release. Now my story unfolds through the rhymes and rhythms of spoken word & poetry. So, find a comfortable spot to retain, relax and read as you explore an adventure on the "Land of Milk & Honey B."

My name is Bridgette Craine, my alias name is "Honey B". I lost both "paRENTs" a year apart and now "MY ANGEL" watches over me. Since, I was a kid I was addicted to the "WHITE STUFF". Food was my comfort, but my worst enemy. You see I never dated because I had a poor relationship with "FOO'D". I took part in the ole "JEALOUSY" trait when it was obvious I didn't fit in!! The last thing I wanted to hear about was "THE RING"! Eventually, it became noticeable I needed to exercise, "F.A.C.T.!!" Although, I did lose weight over time my "REJECTION" made me pause, and rewind into the familiar feeling and I was back at "I LOVE YOU, though". Then, my "SMILE" lost its "CHEERS". I was a "BROKEN WOMAN" with overwhelming "ANXIETY". I need "W.E.", I couldn't do it alone. My "ABILITY" had "DEMENTIA" I lost myself "JEREMIAH 29:11" and seemed to have forgot my "PIECE OF PEACE".

My hands found a new adventure & "writing it out, until it was right out" flowed my feelings from the pain, to the pen & pad…

PaRENTs

If I had ownership of when u could go...

You both would live forever and never go!

Mommy and Pops I'm still here conquering through each day...

Your absence in my mind I try to block away....

I wish I could go back and keep you here with me....

Like move in my place and just simply be...

It's hard sometimes not seeing y'all face...

I guess GOD decided it was time to end the race...

Here on earth, thanks for giving me birth...

I hope I make you proud...

I promise to keep GOD first with my feet on solid ground...

We are all just renting time in this world...

I can't wait to see y'all again...

I'm still your treasured pearl!

My Angel

Some days are better than others...

It's hard at times to accept life's journey without you mother...

I tend to block out thoughts of you...

So, I don't breakdown, but get through...

The hurt goes deep, if you only knew...

Life isn't & never will be the same...

The support system of GOD with others, along with prayers, keeps

me mentally sane...

I've often had no sunshine, after the rain..., BUT when I cry out for

help GOD sends an Angel to help me maintain...

Mother, please keep watching over me, as your child...GOD I ask you

let her be my guardian angel for a long while...

I love you Mama.

White Stuff

I'm Addicted to the white stuff, you know you done had it before it's

got a kick to it and will have you craving for more...

Comes in a bag for a reasonable price...

Too much of it will have you up all night...

Gives a boost of high energy with excitement the brain has

overwhelming connects of enticement...

One spoonful, just isn't enough you want more and more until body

responds clearly, "stop this stuff"...

Can give you a headache if you overdose, maybe even take out a

kidney, but who knows...

The pleasures of it are temporary, the over usage of it can be scary,

or deadly...

Moderation is key, it's in every edible thing you eat & drink...

Can't avoid it with fast food, so addictive your tongue may be

"immune" so your limits can't be established because it's in your

favorite foods...

When you see it, you grab it and think about it briefly, BUT look at

your need for it and pursue immediately...

I'm addicted to sugar.

Foo'd

I have a bad relationship, I know I need 2 let it go...

It breaks me down SLOWLY, & humiliates me BOLDLY...

Could it be that it chose ME...Hold up... it doesn't even know ME!!

I introduced myself, next thing I know it's on my PALATE, and I feel I

can't live without IT...

Saturated, in its seasonings...falling for its FLAVORS...Getting

another plate needs to be WAIVERED...

It's a corrupt, comfort...a daunted date...my tasteful, toxic

relationship with food that remains on my PLATE.

I better wake up before its 2 LATE!

Jealousy

Comparing and competing to have finer things running a race that means nothing at all...

I want, I need, I have to have...

NO! You thought, you don't, you wish you had...

Vision so, blurred you can't see you have more than enough...

Truth be told at your last breathe your possessions will be someone else's stuff...

The best things in life are free...

You can't get real love, joy, peace, wisdom, and happiness with currency...

If you can buy who you are, you won't last, foundation like glass soon to shatter fast...

God meant to "Gel-Us-You-See?"

Love one another not hate so, let's soak and indulge in truth because we can all break bread & there's enough food for everyone's plate...

Soooo, why are you hating? Are your blessings not waiting?

You claim to have faith, you speak things into existence, but the jealousy in your soul has you with some resistance...

What's for them is for them, and what's for you is for you...

You can't follow someone else's heart and your own too...

So, WAKE UP, WAKE UP!

You only get one shot and don't waste time granted for wishes "un-got" because of jealousy.

The Ring

When will I get married? A question I'm asked, OFTEN...

What's the rush??? I've only seen a few successful "arrangements of

forever love" that last before the COFFIN...

What happened to being friends, building a bond and getting to

know one another before tying the KNOT?

You don't really know a person until close synergy, then you'll have

solid standards on whether to marry them, or NOT...

My mechanisms keep me protected in my EYES... So, any situation

with dating won't come as a SURPRISE...

I can't handle much, or maybe I don't want TO....Irritates me how

some guys, say " I want YOU".... You don't know what you want

besides physical fantasies and monetary GAINS...

I can't open myself to the disruptive chaos, so my reservations

REMAIN.... I'd be a fool to entangle myself in your aimless GAMES...

You don't want me for reasons I PERFER... You want a toy to play with, someone to use and emotionally abuse & I'm just not HER....

Where are the real gentlemen? You know the ones that keep God first, open doors, and says kind words for reassurance MATTERS...even suggest personal meetings over cellular phone, or social media DATA...

He's really digging you, not seeking to be a sinful BATTLE. When someone asks me this, I admit, I cringe internally. My mind races and my heart skip's a BEAT and my anxiety elevates and I feel WEAK...

I've wondered the answer to this question and now I think I know it. I'm not ready. I need healing and I can't handle let-DOWNS. So, I'll invest in myself and allow God to heal me deep down for NOW....in the mist of this my Prince will ABOUND.

14

𝒥.𝒜.𝒞.𝒯

(F)luffy (A)nd (C)ycled the 20mile (T)rail)...

Intimidation added with deep efforts to do something I'd never

DONE! Seeing all the people with biker bodies that rode a 100 miles

for FUN...

The discouragement tried to distract my destiny...

Here I was a plus-size woman on a ONE speed beach cruiser, no

gears to shift at ALL...

My eagerness and determination kept me on board, even though my

confidence staggered to FALL...

At the start of the race I cried. I was riding alone until the first rest

stop then, I seen a familiar FACE...

My internal energy boosted and I was ready to continue at a steady

PACE...

I didn't have a helmet that fit my HEAD. I had on layers of clothes for

comfort that I soon had to SHRED...

I was overheating and the discomfort of the seat had me wanting to

walk INSTEAD...

15

I had to keep my head up, think positive and follow the leader
AHEAD...

 The hills made me work my leg muscles in areas I had forgot where
THERE...

The wind blew against me and that created a speck of FEAR...

10miles in...I couldn't give up after coming to this place right HERE,
so the journey continued...

The views were full of nature and captured my PAIN...

I forgot I was hurting and refocused on the GAIN...

Giving up was an option I just didn't CHOOSE it...

 I had a dear friend push me when I felt deeply challenged and like I
would LOSE it...

The lesson of a helping hand in a time of NEED, hit me hard as I
caught a "charlie horse" in my upper thighs and KNEES...

20 miles done, the battle of fear has been FOUGHT...

Victory is mine and a lesson has been TAUGHT.

BELIEVE IN YOURSELF!!

Rejection

Steaming from my childhood...I've been injected with something that

pumps in my blood EVERYDAY...

No matter how hard I may try to avoid it, it flows through my blood

ANYWAY...

The toxicity of its existence shows up in many WAYS...

Often, times it makes me isolate, and watch the days pass AWAY...

I'm aware of its presence, and dislike its RESERVATIONS...

It needs to get vaccinated out, but for many reasons it gains another

'veined' ROUTE...

I need treatment to heal, so I can have purer BLOOD, My 'line' has a

connection with this liquid redness that at times has no LOVE...

It's my (INJECTION) of REJECTION that caused an INFECTION...

Which is why I call out to GOD for my

CORRECTION before, my character is corrupted....

I need his PROTECTION to heal my REJECTION.

Read Before Love

I love you though...

Looks can be deceiving go ahead read this poetic expression, before

the misleading...

You make me feel, so good...

Your around when I'm alone, you warm me up when I'm cold...

You are nice to me; you listen and always help me ease my mind...

You are full flavor when marinated; taste better with time...

The way your presence makes me glow...

It's sad to see you have to leave, when you go...

I know you can't stay forever, forever isn't forevermore...

As time twirls, things change, never stay the same anymore.

Your taste is different, and your seasonings are in a certain way...

I have a poor relationship with food, you can tell that if you read

this today.

Smile

The matter of one's heart is a reflection of their outward endeavors...

A man's action never lies and shows where he/she may need to get it together...

I dislike when people don't smile. It causes wrinkles and takes more muscles to weigh the face down...

You're blessed if your 6ft above the ground, not sure why people entertain longevities of frowns...

Smiles create positive mentions. Happiness gets a position, and the love in the day gets carried away on a mission...

Smiles intertwined with love are powerful when it happens, all behind a smile of a courageous person with joyful heart tapping...

It's free, but comes with a high price a smile can change a mood, desire, and heart that was turning to dark, not light...

Always be aware of your part in this experience of the day, let your

smile be the voice when you don't what to do, or what to say...

Smiles are contagious, beautiful, and outrageous! The effects of a

simple smile are simply, amazing!!

Cheers

My joy past all understanding has my peace in high demand...

The strength in my soul keeps me standing with a spiritual freedom

above any man...

No interruptions to the abundance of lavish laughter, putting the

pathway in place and order...correction master

I've learned to enjoy life... It's taken me some years. I use to be

dependent on the cheers of my peers... now my sight of reality has

overcome all opinioned steers...

I am who I am, so grab a seat and watch if u want...CHEERS! I've

made up my mind to face and erase space for any and all fears!

Broken Woman

A broken woman has potential outside of the norm, calm one

minute, the next a roaring storm...

Her direction has no lead you won't know what hit you, her mind no

ease she's coming to get you...

Be careful how you treat her and never abuse, or beat her, Karma is

her best friend and she's guaranteed to meet yah...

It's true, what goes around comes around and how you are, is what

you attract harsh reality, of hard facts. Gravity connects with the

character and establishes a conclusion, defined definition of YOU...

a true loser.

Anxiety

Why do I even fool with you? It serves no meaningful PURPOSE...I'm constantly undermined & downplayed made to feel WORTHLESS...

You don't listen to me. Communication is out the DOOR. You paralyze my responses and fog my mind even MORE...

When we first met I didn't know you, so I went with the FLOW...

I've learned now to not do that, so I know when to stay or, let GO...

This relationship has lasted so LONG. I've been doing life with you and feel very lost and ALONE...

It's time I take the reins of my redemption BACK... Captivate my life's experience just like THAT...

You made decisions for me with or, without my PERMISSION...

My victim mentality has me wandering with no mental AMMUNITION...

How does one get away from ANXIETY & PANIC ATTACKS... that captures their senses to their CORE?

I personally, don't have an answer just yet, so I'll rest in my writings along with prayer and in GOD'S RESERVOIR!

1800-662-HELP #1Peter 5:7

W.E.

W.E. are...

The life breathers for 9 months...The population wouldn't "pop" without us...

Our soul holds a soul that we hope to hold, as the flesh is created inside our mold...

W.E. are...

Natural Nourishes...

Humbled Helpers...

Caring Correlations...

Precise Protectors...

W.E. are...

Fearfully and wonderfully made... created by the Creator of all nations, dominions & domains...

HE is the same ONE that created us in our mother's womb and knew us before we had a name, in tune... Psalms 139:14

W.E. are...

Full of integrity, smart, and divine...ready to make a nickel into a dime...if we hit a hard time...Even, in rain we shine...

"W.E." are... Woman of Empowerment!!!

Ability

I'm NOT better than anyone and I KNOW it, and GOD created us all different don't BLOW it...rather SHOW it! Actions speak louder than words....Can't nobody do it like YOU, so do just that and press through. Stored up knowledge to gain your best, letting change take its course as far as the east is to the west! Your allowing vulnerability to conquer through with your abilities that were once "dis..ABLE..d"...and overcoming fears that once "en...ABLE..d" because in the middle of it all your ABLE!

DeMENtia

I love how green the trees are and how the sun shines, it brings back memories for me, you know rewinds time...

My mind goes in and out , I forget more than I'd like I don't always understand what you say to me, often I don't know my days from nights...

Confusion overloads my thoughts and stress penetrates the rate of my heart, I become anxious and find I don't know who I am, or even "where I are"...

It's clear you don't understand me and don't know my disease. Calm down and get to know me, with loving patience and comforting ease...

Life is totally different, puts perspectives in alignment. My health was my wealth, the whole time. I'm nothing without my mental finding...

So, take today as a key to unlock the many doors of life, treasure

the values you find as you correct your wrongs to right...

Time lives for no man, and detoured health care can stagger any

plan, I have dementia. I hope one day you understand.

Jeremiah 29:11

"For I know the plans I have for you"(Jer. 29:11)...is what HE

SAID...

 I'm glad he reminded me because I forgot & felt my future was

DEAD...

INSTEAD I have HOPE when doubt tries to poke... NOPE! My head is

up and my shoulders are BACK, ready with armor of GOD (Eph. 6:11),

set for any and all ATTACKS! The angels hear my cry and come in

PACKS! I'm redeemed and that's a FACT!

Piece of Peace

I can live without a piece of me, but I can't function without a peace in me...

The trade of pieces for no peace, torments existence deep in me...

Peace is priceless and should be protected, give it away if you want to and you'll regret it...

Everyone wants a piece of you, but no one contributes to the peace in you...

Synergy is real, keep like mindsets close...

If the shoe doesn't fit, walk away, let it go...

Your peace has a place and pace, don't let peace robbers come near, or invade your space.

Bell Of Tell

Everyone watches, some want you to fail! Every wonder how you could have 300 likes and 20 views what does that tell?

People compete in silence, while hiding their hate, when success still hits, they fall in love with that undeniable jealousy trait.

Many will swear they are the reason you made it, truth be told your journey you created!

Credit for someone else's success, is like denying yourself, in front of yourself ONLY to still be yourself!! Worry about self!

You don't see the behind the scenes challenges, battles and setbacks. You see the outcome and tell yourself "You want that!"

The success seen on the scene isn't easy, or free. Time was of the essence, before the complete.

Feet planted, mental on strong, leaning back ringing the bell of tell, sounding the Alarm!

30

Fri-Enemy

You want me to engage in your thoughts?

So, you want me to disregard my mind for yours?

You sound like a fool voicing crazy noise!

If I don't know anything else, I'm a leader from start.

Originally, in my veins pumping creativity to my heart.

You want to distract what you can't destroy, feeling challenged God

has me with a purpose and I'm not easily influenced anymore.

You can't use the same tactics there useless and out the door, never

seen the tables turning on you before.

We don't wear the same shoe size, you couldn't walk a mile in my

shoes, only give taunted instructions on where to go, and how to's.

True friends seek to help, not harm. I'm now changed heart guarded

and somewhat armed.

Treat people how you want to be treated and open your eyes, you have something unethical and corrupt on the inside.

That needs soul surgery, before you commit another burglary. You

joy robbing, no loving, misguided friend...

Hopefully, you get healing, from the deep hole within.

Power of a Mirror

The power of a mirror, and it's reflection of truth...

It'll answer questions you have no answers to...

Self-correction seems to be so hard, especially when your hurt,

damaged, or scarred...

The power of a mirror, and it's reflection of truth...

Don't look at it, if you enjoy the false fabrications you have about

you...

The truth does bring pain, but trust you can get through anything

that shouldn't sustain...

Watch the company you keep, some if not many may not want you to

gain...

Afraid their efforts will be in overlooked or, downsized claims...

"Some bodies" need a mirror, it'll tell their story... and when that

raw reveal releases, we'll see who really gets the glory...

Toxic people, usually tell on themselves because "everyone is toxic,

BUT them... what the hell???"

Poisonous tongues with angelic faces, one of the many reasons for

resorts to isolation...

The eyes of a man lets you see inside without a vibe...something's

you just can't run from or, hide...

The power of a mirror, and it's reflections of truth...

It'll answer questions and have facts about the authentic, real you!

Washed Up

Gather. Sort. Wash. Dry & FOLD....the process of laundry we all KNOW...

Some do it monthly, many do it WEEKLY....Depending on their schedule, & when time is FREELY!

The "Unstoppable" beads, gives the laundry a soft scented BREEZE! Now, the owner's nasals can "Snuggle" the aroma w/EASE.

A "Tide" of strength to "Gain" the "Purex"(purest) form of our "All". "Oxi-Clean" gives off an "Arm & Hammer" feel that "Woolites" us ALL.

The "Joy" of "Xtra" clean "FAB"rics after a good WASH...put them in the dryer w/some "DOWNY" & make em' SOFT!

Smell the magic happen, and touch it real SOON! The softness will put you in a deep sleep like when you were curled in the WOUND! lol "CLOROX" bleaches out odors & stains that "Surf" in laundry and are BOUND...I've just given you a poetic descriptions of laundry PRODUCTS, DETERGENT, and SOFTNERS that are in stores 2 be FOUND...

"BOUNCE" to get an ounce of some "lavish liquid" SOAPS... or , "power powder"...as i "SHOUT" that's all FOLKS! LOL

Giving-Thanks

Hours of preparation, no sleep the night (before)...

Soon to have family & friends coming through the (door)...

A warming home of happiness for hours, and even (days)...

The aroma of a sweet ham cooking, along with a honey (glaze)...

The smell of the prepared feast makes the stomach (growl), the eyes

move in amazement like "(wow)"...

The "giving of thanks" for this time of (year), a family oriented

holiday full of lavish love and joyful (cheer)...

Board games, music, cards, and (dominoes)...

Enjoying the created memories & moments as the day (flows)...

Breaking bread over laughter, while chatting until the yawns

(appear)...

The sign of yet, another successful Thanksgiving (year), that can be

reminisced over from this place right (here)... the heart.

Not Everyone

I've learned NOT everyone is for you...

For most the season is short, and will eventually, end. Especially, if

it's toxic, and you can't breathe from within...

A season changes like people do. You have to change with it, or you

risk your physical, emotional, and mental...

The same interests, doesn't necessarily mean long term

connections...

God, I thank you for giving me discernment way before the life

learned lessons...

Don't get me wrong I'm sociable and like to have fun, with a

requirement of rejuvenation and isolation...

NOT everyone is for YOU...

Hush Hurt

ALERT!! This is another transparent piece that annoys my peace!

My STATE makes a STATEment, Actions louder than

words...Experiences have made me an emotional stuffer, voice

silenced and unheard...

#silent killer

Participations of manipulations out raged feelings toward the

situations...

#corruption before the eruption

The deep rooted disconnect, resting doormat in daunted distractions,

random outbursts from built up, unexpressed reactions.

#loyal loneliness

I've learned how to be passive aggressive, it's became a learned

behavior, so others respect my presence now than later...

#Defensive Dignity

My destiny isn't determined by their dysfunction, think before you

speak, be calm, and hangout in your peace before the beast gains a

release don't give these dynamics a lease...

#character construction

JESUS can you heal me from the hurt that I feel deep in the depth,

this season of stagnation, hasn't been conquered,

yet...

#Saved by the Savior

Fake Love

I loved you more than myself...

When around you I couldn't see anyone else...

You made me glow like none other...

I wanted you more than a friendship; I was seeking to go further...

You were my sweet, poison that tasted "oh, so good"...

I was dying for your attention on a level that only I understand...

My tender toxicity, the medicine to the void that resided, within me to be loved by you...

The aroma of your pores made me take deep breathes more and more...

Hypnotized by your senses, I was captured by your love spells, for sure...

Gone mentally behind you, couldn't stand a site without you...

You made me feel like I could soar in mid-air...I knew it was fake love, but didn't care...

Whatever affection you dispensed I grabbed without a mess...

My low self-esteem played a role in all, of this. Now that I love

myself, it's all been dismissed...

I'll never forget you though...

You were the best fake love; you made it feel real...

I'm glad I woke up before it was too late...

Fake feelings grabbing my heart for a toxic take...

Stay focused, it's worth the wait!

Know You

I want to get to know you...

The invaluable contributions of spending time, with one another...

Not knowing if you're meant for me, if I should keep this connection going further...

I want to get to know you...

It's too early in the correlating condition to determine the position, all I really know is, I'm seeking eventual "marriage on a mission"...

I want to get to know you...

The investments of conversations & mental penetrations...

The butterflies in my stomach, causing my heart to start ah' racing...

I want to get to know you...

Let my guard down before you...

You seem to be the one, I simply adore you...

I want to get to know you...

You're a gentleman, that's sweet and still open doors. You assure me, you enjoy my company and personality even more...

I want to get to know you...

Can this be real? Does this type of man still exist, it's cuffing season and I'm trying to get a diamond bracelet on the wrist... LOL

Bully Me Not

So, you mean to tell me...

You think I'm going to sit back and take your attack... I take on a lot

of things, but this is not that!

Yep, I'm going to speak my peace, and if it comes to it make your

grip with gravity cease...

I know I've changed, I use to allow ignorance to have its way, but I

woke up and like "burger King"... I'm having it my way... My way,

my day... After this battle you'll be calling "may day may day"...

I told you to back up, but you didn't wanna listen now you're running

away from the one you ran up on... Bullying stops with me... Now,

carry on...

Oh, you thought I was playing because my humble, humor still

exists...

I done told you once, I'm not allowing you, but continue at your own

risk...

It's said, "a scary person will kill you"...

Well, so will one that "said what they said", but you wouldn't kneel

to my request and now an outcome awaits you, so gone head...

Lives gone, behind a person with a void... Something/Someone hurt

them, but it could have all been avoid-(ed), and their joy restored in

(side)...

The affirmation of attention, did I mention love, a hug, some sort of

affectionate tug... I've told you before "love is a powerful

expression"...let's try & discontinue bullying, and start

expressing...LOVE!

So, you mean to tell me...

Be Smart

Are you "obsessed with the possess?" You won't ever get my

character to waiver... let me dismiss this mess before I counterfeit

my behavior...

Why do you have such a cold heart without reflection of the cost...?

Your interruption will be interceded, actions taken before the lost...

I'm far from scary, but have too much to lose... I'm one to do a

"toss 'n' turn"...you know... "Sleep without a snooze". #Knockout.

Are you crazy, are your trying to get one of yours (eyes) turned

lazy? You can't see straight it's clear... I'm not a confrontational

type, but I won't back down from a fight. Let me make that clear...

The chaos you created is my fault?

Sounds crazy, stupid, and wild...

Please tell me why you came for me. "Wooow!" How do u know I

don't speak to ignorance, but trigger the... "pooooow?"

You're a reason I sometimes reject my personality... it attracts different people to want to be around me... It's all good I won't change... If necessary I'll take my time and aim at the target in range...

I need you to "Be Smart"!!

Wake Up

There's nothing more powerful than a changed mind...

There's something more purposeful, than wasting time...

You have to meditate, reevaluate, and reconstruct your viewpoint on life...

Stresses of the world will blemish your sight, if God's not on site to get it right...

How can I expect God's strength, if I don't stand on his standards?

You can't poison the well and complain about the water, get it together...

Draw a bloodline (in the name of Jesus), fight back and watch the favor follow...

Don't be delusional to the facts of truth. Dig deep, research, and find the roots in YOU that have grown hallow...

Growing pains are a real experience we all have faced, don't live in regret because the past you can't erase...

It's time to make space for a new adventure...Wake up the eyes of your heart it's gonna be an elevated level with higher potential.

Let Me

Let me tell you what happened...

I fell asleep with peace while napping...

Woke with joy in my veins & positivity on the brain...

I can guarantee you, God has broken some chains...

My energy is on high & depression on low...

Internal happiness and calmness exposed no stop, but go...

I'm grateful for my sanity & encouraged by His care...

I know I'm not alone, He's omnipotent & omnipresent, always here...

Leading, loving, and letting me, letting me have free will...

So, my pursuit to follow His lead is not fake, but genuinely real...

Woke up from this dream, only to be living what my eyes seen...

Let me stand up in my truth, as I stand back and let God lead...

Let me tell you what happened!!

Un-Stuck

New me, where do you be?

You seem to be hiding, intimidated by what you may see...

Your holding on to the familiar, change is a challenge...

Take some deep breathes, slow down, and find some balance...

No one or nothing last forever, your best life is close, so spread out

you're "life -lifting", feathers...

Fly high, soar and enjoy the view...

This journey is customized, ordained, and created for you...

Of course, the struggles real, but it's a part of change...

You keep holding on, your breakthrough is near & already been

arranged...

There's power in vision, and what you say ahead...

The new you is here, to assure the old you has fled...

You can change its fine, what's life without growth anyway, I know...

LEFT BEHIND

Swing

A diamond in the rough with fire to your feet, you have bases to conquer outside of defeat...

The pitcher leaning back to possibly, throw a curve ball...

You're focused, ready, looking & standing tall...

You hold the "bat for battles" for unknown forces coming your way...

Unsure of the impact you raise your arms back & take a-swing anyway...

Striiiike!!! You missed the opportunity to make a play, you're not quitting though, so u plant your feet and stay...

Ok, here we go again, same stance different moment let's try for a win. The sweat rolling on your face makes your adrenaline pick up pace again...

After all, you could hit a homerun and have to step on every base.

Chewing up the failures, spitting out discouragement written all over

your face...

If eyes could talk, mine would be talking spit, the residue of my

saliva hits the ground before the possible "big hit"...

Here goes nothing, I close my eyes, put mighty force into the swing,

taking chances, and the ball takes a high rise...

2 my surprise, it's a HOME RUN!!!

I circled the diamond on the field, in disbelief, one strike and several

tries, don't give up KEEP HOPE ALIVE...let your determination speak

on the "when, where, and why's"...

A diamond in the rough with fire to my feet, you have bases to

conquer outside of defeat!!

Let's Talk About It

Look I have to stand in my truth! Freedom awaits my arrival and the destiny in my soul craves more than just survival! It's time for a personal intervention, a resurrected revival...

What's done in the dark always comes to the light...

The Conscience nudges, and awakens the soul to get up, and get it right...

Aright! I'm up, but why do I have to make this change. I'm comfortable and really don't wanna go through this hurt, of correcting pain...

If you never face the failures, bitterness, or unforgiving feelings...

it'll get a free ride to destroy, make a choice to diminish it...

Let's start with lust! It's foul! You can't trust & makes the soul rust!

Leave this demonic, destroying spirit alone it's a must! Envision life on a higher level before you return back into dust!!(Ecclesiastes 3:20)

Snakes replace the real with the fake & can make the mind double,

unbalance in a toxic space! They are sneaky, & not worth much to

have. Can deplete the soul of the prominent position it once had, it's

sad...

I'm use to carrying burdens deep in my soul. GOD, wait!

This weight is too heavy to hold. You see I like to have control even

it weighs me down, breaking me into pieces, crumbling on the

ground...

Why would you be so, foolishness to not follow HIS word? It's there

for reason and without it you will have tough life lessons to learn...

I don't have an answer that would justify my behavior... I'm just a

woman trying to go through life, regain myself in areas not right,

change my ways... continued waiver...

Lost in the conflictive battle, on the long and narrow path

Spiritual warfare constantly bringing me defeating, challenging

raft...

Save yourself the trouble and humble your ways, or risk having

harder, than easier days! GOD fights your battles and has it under

control. You just grab His promises and trust HIM wholeheartedly, as

the chaos unfolds. (Proverbs 3:5-6)

John Ch.11

Bridgette, come forth! You are alive not living amongst the dead.....Your lungs are compressing and I said what I said...

(Lazarus)

Stay woke! Gag up... no hope! Life will pass you by, get a grip, before that last shut eye...listen to my truth don't follow the lie....

The gate of gloom makes you repeat cycles, going in circles, not squares... flat TIREdness , no SPARES, collection of exaggerated fears... fears of letting go, fears of change, give it to GOD he has power to rearrange!

He is way maker, promise keeper, almighty, the way, truth and life he is the master mind when it comes to making wrongs right!!!

Bridgette, come forth! You are alive not living amongst the dead.....Your lungs are compressing and I said what I said...

(Lazarus)

Covid-19

Y'all know this virus has a cure...

If you're scared pray and grab some scriptures that lay near...

You know the HEALER, and how HE gets down...

He's put breathe in the dead and makes diseases of all types do a

turnaround... Can you hear me now?

Shutting down the world is impossible... you may slow down some

operations, but nothing will stop it...

How can one shutdown something they didn't create...

What really needs to be heard for our livelihood sake...?

Labels reveal this virus isn't new....

Why all the panicked purchases like it's the last thing to do...?

Don't let the news make u panic...

Simply have common sense with this pandemic...

The news anchors will hype u up with exaggerated emotions...

Let the anchor of GOD keep u steady and peacefully floating...

HE has it and always will...

Let your peace NOT be shaken, you don't control when u go... May

as well live...

C.O.V.I.D. 19...Can't Overpower the Victorious Indefinite Designer...

Even u tried 19 times. Lol

D.N.A" (Do Not Allow)

My DNA has been tweaked, my Do Not Allow (D.N.A.) policies

released...

Why do I even be bothered? No man has time to waste considering;

we are all on God's time, plan, & grace...

Always trying to please the next, and forgetting of self, emptiness

awaits and it's something else...

You will never be enough if all you have wasn't, that's hard facts,

tough reality of acceptance of it...

Why am I the way I am, heart, so big yet, I seem to always get the

shorter hand...

My revised D.N.A. will reject all that's without sense, self-care is a

must for correction of the mental exist...

Let me get some space, kneel down on my face, and figure out why

my D.N.A. Policy seems invisible, limited trace...

Do Not Allow yourself to go in a downward mental space; it has no

place of positive outcomes, only negative registrations to face...

We are all unique, there will never be an exact other, only copy cats

of the original DNA governed...

My DNA has been tweaked, my Do Not Allow (D.N.A.) policies

released.

Soaring Soul

I AM because HE SAID I was....

I WAS because HE SAID I am....

PLANNED, ORDAINED purpose...

ORDAINED, PURPOSE planned...

Differently, DESIGNED for HIS GREATER GOOD...

Perfectly, ALIGNED, yet often MISUNDERSTOOD...

SPIRITUAL endeavors...

PRAYERS to hold it all together...

My ROCK I stand on...

My HOPE when I feel alone...

I'm sure all will work out for the BETTER...

A BIRD with a broken wing ready to FLY....

JESUS you're my GPS across the SKY...

I don't worry about my SHELTER...

NOR, any of my FOOD...

You created it all, so I know I'll be COOL...

Unknown territories across the PLAINS...

Freedom to spread my wings & soar and manage to MAINTAIN...

My trust is in you, always will BE. You're my protector and provider

and you constantly prove that to ME...

One Thing

One thing I knew, but needed to reapply is to not EVER compromise my peace, for someone's invited apply...

People pleasing is a horrible trait to have and practice, has no beneficial outcomes, and generally leaves to pleaser empty and unhappy...

What you may want, doesn't feel right, signs of the soul that can't be taken lite...

Learning to let folks be mad if they want to be upset, due to control being forfeited, your peace is priority to protect...

Respect is earned not given, a must departure for those who don't indulge in it...

Voiced views, "knows and knews", put yourself above all the tactics of being cheated, or misused...

One thing I knew, but needed to reapply is to not EVER compromise my peace, for someone's invited apply.

U.F.C.

(Underlying Find of Character)

Life's defenders, opposing contenders... you fight the opponents, KO
(knock out) possible winner...

You never know if the blow is a defeating go, the opponent of
opposition may remain despite, your mighty flow...

Staring in the eyes of your energized enemy, in exchange for a full
throttle of throw outs, conquering, releasing for the battle of gainful
epiphany...

They say practice makes perfect, well training keeps you prepared;
no matter the techniques used the defensive operations are instilled
there...

The brass bass of the sound in the crowd, hearing the roars aloud,
as the lights flash with illumination all around...

A hydration of liquids, the dripping of sweat, mouth piece in, feeling strong, no turning back or, fret...

Bouncing on my feet up and down we go, building up my stamina before I let go...

Release of the beast, I can't contain myself...Challenges and defeat's, have grown my internal wealth...

Unlike how I use to be and near to who I'll become, self reflections of fresh restarts, mentally analyzed to come...

Facing the facts and overcoming the attacks... a justified fight obtaining confidence lacks!...

In the UFC (Underlying Find of Character)....

Snap-Out

I've lost myself. Deeply lost myself...

How do you find the very one you are?

Should I hide behind materials things, though it's a cover up and won't get me very far?

Maybe I should dance this off in circles, looking square, depressed about the pyramid effect of life and how it's just not fair?

Ok...ok, let's be clear I'm going to be fine, just a minor setback with wishes of rewinding of time...

Sometimes moving on, and forward is a challenge, comfort advertises the emotional relaxes, of the past that was grounded Growth has its influences and has to happen. Life will be mediocre is nothing changes around it...

Granted something's and people will remain the same consistency isn't always key, if it hinders the pinnacles your plan to reach... some day.

For-THE-Give" (Forgiveness)

I'm..."for-THE-give" (forgiveness)

Forgiving of others is essential to your spiritual growth...

It's vital that you stand in your truth, & find your peace like you're under oath...

Choose to make an agreement with reality to create solutions, & level up...

Go ahead and change your mind, attitude, & heart...You know "better up"...

Unforgotten, forgiveness is one the most power things a hurting heart can do...

Keep in mind un-forgiveness is a defeating act that only rots and torments YOU...

Don't allow your subconscious mind to imprint, impressions on your conscious mental corrections...

Nor, allow the divine element of rest (sleep), to be dominated by the consumption's of ignorance...

I admit I was wrong, ownership of faults. Lessons learned, earned, experienced, and taught...

Being the bigger person is priceless, character correction bought...

Less tension, less battles, more life setbacks, fought...

I'm "for-THE-give" (forgiveness).

Purpose

(Jeremiah 1:5)

Speaks on the past tense...

Before, the speck of existence...

The formation of creation...

Our parents made us; God formed and created us...

We are:

Built by design...

Crafted for a calling...

Wired for work...

Made with purposeful involvement...

Purpose requires participation to endure our destined, destination...

What if GOD let you live in, all you believe in?

Would your life have manifestation?

How strong is your faith?

Do you still have hope?

Can you speak on God's blessings, or has your voice of life been provoked?

Fire inside gone....smoked out, choked up down to the bone...

You're blinded by the fogs of frustration, so open the eyes of your heart...

You're fearfully and wonderfully made true, facts to NEVER part...

(Psalms 139:14)

They Said

They said...

They has no identified names...

Only open random, manipulated information...

How foolish and lame...

No facts, maybe lies, no evidence just a waste of time, to even

repeat...

No matter what they said, what you said is all they will speak...

He lies in the middle of tHEy...

No! He said it because it wasn't me...

Look at you trying to take back, what you said...

When you should of kept our mouth closed from the beginning...

Now, that's what they said...

Cost

They say love doesn't cost a thing, but that's a lie...

I've had my heart broken & crushed triggering a soul

cry...

You see sometimes love is pain you lose more than you

gain...

That creates feelings of hurt, bitterness, & shame...

Shoot, I want that kind of love that makes me float...

That kind of love that's pure love, full of happiness and

genuine hope...

Love is such a very powerful expression...

True love comes with boundaries, balance, and an

understood level of perceptions...

Now affections... it'll make you feel like you're in love...

You know the "love vs. lust" factor...

This is where the statement of "Only time will tell" comes

into practice & lust it doesn't stay **HONEY** it comes to play

HONEY, it gets what it wants and gets out the way

HONEY...

So, love does cost a thing be prepared, but try...

Your reactions to the attractions determine who you

spend it with and why...**LOVE COSTS.**

Short, Simple, Sweet Drip...

Eyesight

Chew'd Up Chats

Lil' Light

Hi-Go

Custom Communication

I Jus' Wanna

Eyesight #SSS

Laws of the land...

Broken and bended...

Lives changed forever...

Predictions unknown, limited...

Color does matter, always has...

White isn't always pure, and colored isn't always bad...

Some will get mad, maybe even become surprised...

I'm just sharing a snippet of the characteristics I've seen through my

observations in eyes of...

The shredding of blood, political distractions and lies...tears dripping

down, prayers to the skies.

Chew'd Up Chats #SSS

(Paying me attention doesn't get your bills out of DEBT...

On a scavenger hunt trying to find something negative to COLLECT...

Private chatters and manipulated obscurities over something

WET...choosing to "Let the Fret" ...YET, getting nowhere...

"Chews and news"...gossip is what they call it, with isolated

presences and open MOUTHS, your truthful, lies without facts that

are wicked & WILD...

We have two ears, not two FACES...many get that confused and grab

a mask for the TAKING...

Trying to disguise themselves...don't want to be EXPOSED, foolish

moved mumbled FOES...hoping no one finds out or, even KNOWS.

Lil' Light #SSS

This Lil' light I have... I'm going to let it beam, silence only distracts, downplays, & dims the abundance of dreams...

This Lil' light I have... one day will light up a stadium, no regrets of the ideas I have, but GOD is the one that created 'em...

This Lil light I have... has to go to dark places, depressed spaces... It's hope for all nationalities, all individuals, all races...

This Lil light I have... must be seen. If it's covered, it will lose its effectiveness, reasons, and means...

This Lil light I have... is in my possession with purpose...I have to expose the heavy and lite, so this Lil light isn't made worthless...

This Lil light I have.

ΗI...Go #SSS

Open mind, grinding thoughts...

Creative moves, battles lost...

Don't listen to them, never give up...

Stay encouraged like your following a billion bucks...

Even when it's silent your gift speaks, so...

Stay focused and reaching the pinnacles you plan to reach!!

Custom Communication #SSS

Out of shape, no boxes for me...

More like a creative design with no limits to be...

Ready to conquer the world, change my mind and calculated ways...

Open up my heart, & bleed out on the page...

Red ink to think...

Truth at its finest...

Writing out the pain and pleasure
Rare descriptions without hesitated alignments...

Hush up for what this has to be heard...
So my silence has to be spoken and disturbed.

I Jus' Wanna #SSS

I just wanna live...

Live with purpose...

Purpose not worthless...

Worthless reversed...

Reversed actions not rehearsed...

Rehearsed isn't real...

I'm just writing to give u motivation to "write it out until its right

out" and live.

PoeTRY!!
(Demo Piece for Readers)
Fill In the blank. Answers on last page

Bee Me

The sweet poet, with sticky, entertaining _____

Writing is an addiction...expressions with endless_____

Development of my voice through the penetrating_____

Letting the words form a sentence, allowing my mind to_____

Hiatus Humble Bumble melody, steady forming ideas, to create a better

me.

"Poe-TRY" Page -The indulgence of written and/or spoken expressions with a TRY, as a POET...

(Stick Your Poem Here)

Acknowledgment

First, God thank you for life, itself. I wouldn't be where I am without you and poetry. You know my story better than anyone, and to be able to share pieces of it with the world is an epic expression of excitement!!

Second, I want to thank my parents for making me. I am living in the mist of your absence it keeps my drive taking me places. I miss you both, dearly.

Finally, I want to thank all of my family, friends, and supporters. Your kind words and positive actions keep me buzzing. The sweetness of a soul and the elegance it leaves was motivation for these raw, real, revealing, reads.

"When life stings, know there's honey to soon be seen"

–Honey B

About the Author:

Some say Honey B, but here are details of other parts of
me…

My entertaining name is Honey B Craine…

God and poetry are my outlets to keep my mind sane…

Jane Ross is my mother; William Craine is my father…

both deceased, but my motivation to go further….

Born & raised in Muskogee, Oklahoma…

33yrs old with a college diploma…

Healthcare seems to be the target career choice,

but I loove spoken word, because it gives my soul a
voice…

Laughter is my medicine, love is my cure, always creating
a positive vibe for me & others to endure…

Simply adding pages to my story of life, editing chapters
as my days go by…

What I had planned may be wrong, & not right

God is the author I'm just a character in this book called
life…

Now you have truth and fact of who I am, whose I am,

and where it is I'm going...

My ultimate goal is to simply keep growing...
Choke out fear and throw away doubt, so the world can
see who Honey B Craine is,
and what she's about...
I'm Out!

Thank you for buzzing with me on
the adventure of the sounds & sites of my
life…While on the "wings of the writes"…
At the end of the day I can only be me!!!
You've been given a sweeet dosage of…

"Land of Milk & Honey B."

Bzzzzzzz!!

Word Match Answers:
- ~ words
- ~ curves
- ~ ink
- ~ speak

Made in the USA
Coppell, TX
24 April 2021

54424861R00049